Printed Under License ©2018 Emotional Rescue
www.emotional-rescue.com

Published by Studio Press
An imprint of Kings Road Publishing. Part of Bonnier Publishing
The Plaza, 535 King's Road, London, SW10 0SZ

www.bonnierpublishing.co.uk

Printed in Italy   10 9 8 7 6 5 4 3 2 1

The Wit & Wisdom of

GRANDAD

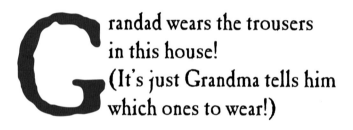

Grandad wears the trousers
in this house!
(It's just Grandma tells him
which ones to wear!)

"**G**randad, Grandma says you haven't lost that old twinkle in your eye... It's just moved to the top of your head."

Grandad liked to spend his free time surrounded by his loved ones. The TV , the TV remote, his TV cup of tea and his TV armchair.

"**S**orry I'm a bit deaf, could you speak up?"
"CAN YOU LEND US A TENNER?"
bellowed his grandchildren.
"Nope, still can't hear you!" said Grandad.

After Christmas, Grandad and Grandma wave their relatives goodbye.

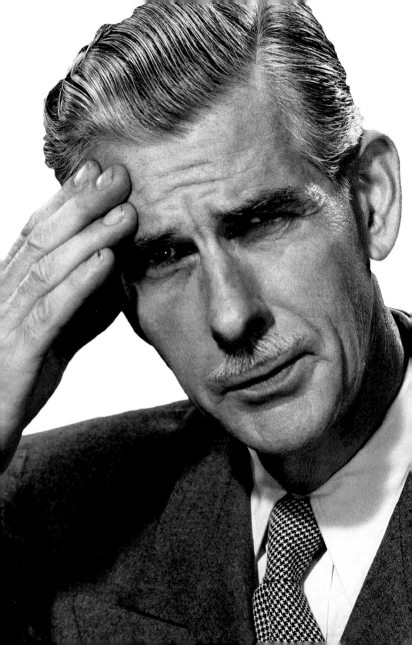

Grandad still had a photographic memory. Unfortunately, it no longer provided same day service.

Grandad hits a hole in one... of his windows.

Just moments too late, Grandad realised it wasn't actually a comode.

"Grandad's asleep, and if he wakes up, he'll put something crap on the telly!"

The stuff looked vaguely familiar and Nan and Grandad sort of remembered having some before the grandkids arrived!

Grandad read the deodorant stick instructions 'Remove top and slowly push up bottom'. It was painful, but his farts smelt lovely!

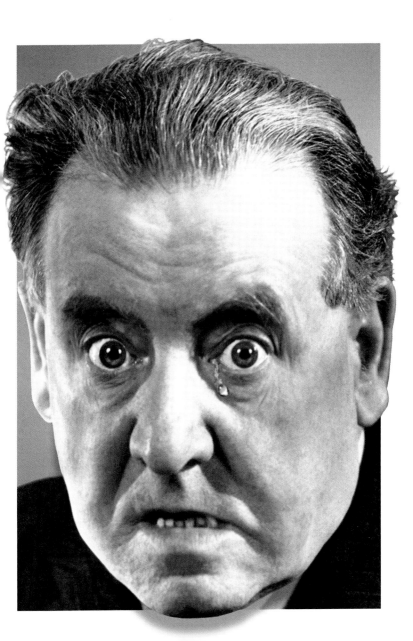

Grandad still hadn't fully grasped this texting lark.

"**O**h #@!% the Archers!"
said Granny to Grandad.
"Let's have some Kanye West!!"

After 4 hours, Edith was beginning to regret asking Grandad what 'offside' meant.

Grandad was having a whole plethora of trouble trying to download apps!

"That's amazing, how did you just say "Sasquatch" without moving your lips?" asked Cecil.
"I didn't!" replied Grandad, "I farted."

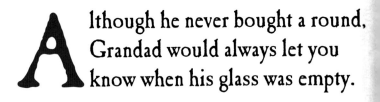

Although he never bought a round, Grandad would always let you know when his glass was empty.

Despite his age, Grandad still found it highly amusing to ring people's doorbells and run away.

"The most expensive part of having grandkids...
is all the beer I have to drink!"

"There's nothing in the world that Grandad can't do... apart from part his hair, obviously!!"

The air rasping out of the balloon really made him laugh because it sounded just like Grandad.

He was the perfect Grandad - he kept his mouth shut and wallet open.

Despite his age, Grandad still went clubbing.

Grandad had got his very own intergrated wordprocessor and printer.
It was called a 'pen'!